What's Next God?

Sandra L. Ross

REJOICE
Essential Publishing

Sandra L. Ross/Rejoice Essential Publishing

PO BOX 512

Effingham, SC 29541

www.republishing.org

Unless otherwise indicated, scripture is taken from the King James Version.'

What's Next God?/Sandra L. Ross

ISBN-13: 978-1-956775-93-8

Dedication

Table of Contents

Acknowledgement

Only God Can...

...you have turned my mourning into dancing for me;
You have taken off my sackcloth and clothed me with
*joy." — **Psalms 30:11***

Introduction

"What's Next God?" was birthed during the 2020 Covid-19 pandemic. Witnessing the financial stressors and being kept in isolation for prolonged periods of time, many marriages were dissolved through divorce, and some tragically became widows. I was speaking at a women's event, and I looked around in the room and so many women were recently widowed and divorced. It was at that moment the Lord gave me the title of this book. He reminded me of my own divorce and how broken I was. While stationed in

Washington state, I attended a Christian *"Divorce Recovery Workshop,"* where I first learned about the five stages of grief. I bought every book about divorce and yet I found myself stuck in my pain. There was no one to talk to because of the hush mentality of a generation that carried over into the church. I felt so alone, shunned, and misunderstood during a challenging time in my life. When I got married, it was forever for me...so I thought. At the end of a relationship, whether it is due to divorce or the loss of a loved one, one must go through the grieving process to know the answer to What's Next God? It is my desire that you, the reader, be encouraged and with my nakedness, you will know the answer to your question, which is Live, Live, Live!!!

CHAPTER ONE:

The Five Stages of Grief

In 1969, Elizabeth Kubler-Ross published *"On Death and Dying,"* discussing the five stages of grief or when coping with death. Her model explained how people experience their own death through terminal illness, which later became the accepted way of understanding grief. The five stages of grief are:

- Denial/Shock
- Anger

- Bargaining
- Depression
- Acceptance

QUESTIONS AND ANSWERS

- What is the purpose of the five stages of grief model?

The model of grief can be a useful tool in identifying and understanding the array of emotions one may experience due to grief.

- Are the Five Stages of Grief in Chronological order?

It is important to note that the five stages of grief model, when first developed, were observed to be experienced by most people in a specific order. However, it is crucial to recognize that grief is a deeply personal journey, and each individual's experience may vary. Some may only go through a few stages, while others may not experience any. This understanding validates the uniqueness of each person's grief experience.

CHAPTER TWO

"Blind Sided" - Denial / Shock

"And when I heard this thing, I rent my garment and my mantle, and plucked off the hair of my head and of my beard and sat down astonished. Then were assembled unto me every one that trembled at the words of the God of Israel, because of the transgression of those that had been carried away: and I sat astonished until the evening sacrifice."— (Ezra 9:3-4 KJV)

Ezra(help/helper) was a Hebrew prophet, priest, and scribe of God. He had a heart for holiness and for the people. He had a passion for biblical truth and authored the books: *Nehemiah, Chronicles, and Malachi.* The Israelites were recently exiled from Babylon and were given specific instructions from God. In this passage, we find Ezra being made aware of the Israelites' activities. In response to what was reported to Ezra, he immediately rips off his garments and pulls out his hair from his head and beard. He then sits down in utter disbelief, and we see this shock manifested. According to Vocabulary.com, shock is defined as, a sudden or upsetting event or experience.

Ezra was in total disbelief that the children of Israel would be disobedient again by intermarrying and leaders were leading the people astray. Ezra sat on the ground without speaking for several hours. The words denial and shock are interchangeable. Denial is when you reject the truth and shock is when the truth is before you, but you are unable to find the logic to support it. Ezra was in denial and did not want to accept the fact that the Israelites sinned again, especially after recently being set free from Babylon. The ripping off of the clothes and his mantle is a symbolic act because he believed in holiness; he did not want a part of their sins. Just like God is holy, we must be holy. Ezra sat on the ground and did not speak for several hours until it was time for sacrifice. Ezra had to process the denial/shock before moving forward with sacrifice. Denial is a self-preservation mechanism that helps you to survive the loss.

I recollect when I heard those dreadful words, "I don't want to be married no more." "I want a divorce." At that minute, those words were playing in slow motion in my mind, and I was no longer in my body. WOW! I did not see that coming. I could not believe it because we had talked about me being transferred to Washington State on spousal duty. We were so excited to spend more time together as newlyweds. That is right, we were married less than a year and dealt with so much separation due to deployments. I beautified our home and cooked Sunday meals every time he came home. We did a lot of excursions and attended church together. I stopped drinking and clubbing and became a chaste wife. That day, my ex-husband called me to tell me he was not coming home for the weekend. This became the norm until that dreadful day when he told me that one woman was not enough for him. How could I contend with that when he had access to all kinds of women from all over the world? I continued to call him to ask if he was coming back and he wouldn't answer the phone, or he would hang up on me.

I was in denial like Sarah in *Genesis 18:15*, *"Then Sarah denied, saying I laughed not; for she was afraid. For he said, Nay; but you didst laugh."* Sarah was well past childbearing age and the angel said she would have a child this time next year. Sarah rejected the truth with everything within her; she couldn't make sense of what was said and the experience to support it as truth. I was numb and continued with life. I got up every day to go to work and I honestly admit I barely remember the repeated phone calls I made because I believed my ex-husband would come back home and we would stay married. I finally was able to speak to him and he repeated he wanted a divorce and when I got off the phone. I heard the still small voice of the Holy Spirit say *1 Corinthians*

7:15-16, "But if the unbelieving departs let him depart. A brother or sister is not under bondage in such cases: but God hath called us to peace."

Then the Holy Spirit spoke to me, *John 14:1, "Let not your heart be trouble; ye believe in God, believe also in me."* It was like I had a spiritual Calgon moment. I was in the eye of the storm. I was enveloped in such a peace and all the chaos of my life was still and silenced. I didn't feel any pain and I wasn't crying. I remember walking everywhere because he took the car. I would walk an hour back and forth to work and to noonday prayer. The church mothers and first Lady kept asking me if I was okay and I said, "Yes." I never lost my praise and smile. Did I say intercession was birthed in me during this time? Let me give you a timeline. On Friday God spoke to me that I was called unto peace and to not let my heart be troubled. On Saturday, I was asked to speak at church on Women's Sunday and God had me reading every scripture about peace.

In comparison, I was Sarah when I kept calling him and pretending my marriage was good. I was also like Ezra; I was blindsided by the fact that my marriage was over before it really had a chance. When I arrived that Sunday morning to speak, I recall the title of my message was, "Hold on to your Peace." *John 14:1 says, " Let not your heart be troubled: ye believe in God, believe also in me."*

The second I opened my mouth, the anointing of God took over and His glory filled the house. It was as if I was in a bubble, and nothing was able to penetrate my peace and joy. Sometimes, I would wonder and question God, "What is this?" I would hear the still small voice of God say, "It is my shalom peace." *John 14:27 says, "Peace I leave with you, my peace I giveth unto you: not as the world giveth, give I unto you. Let not your heart be troubled, neither let it be afraid."* This supernatural peace buffered me from the harsh reality that my marriage was finished and forever wasn't always and forever. This peace enabled me to function in this great turbulent storm. I became a Martha, busy, busy in ministry and it was a band-aid that silenced my pain and kept all the emotions at bay.

CHAPTER THREE

No You Didn't!- Anger

"Be ye angry and sin not: let not the sun go down upon your wrath. Neither give place to the devil." — *(Ephesians 4:26-27 KJV)*

According to Oxford Languages, anger is defined as a strong feeling of annoyance, displeasure, or hostility.

The peace of God initially covered me like a comforter and kept me from losing my mind all the way. It is so true that God knows how much we can bear. I was broken and He gracefully pulled back the cover and I was able to progress to the stage of anger. Let Me Tell You, I Was So Angry! My ex-husband became all kinds of ninjas... and in my Shanae Nae voice and with my hands on my hips, I said, "No You Didn't!" I did everything to be stationed with my ex-husband. I turned down California, Hawaii, and Florida to be with him, which were all prime duty locations. I sacrificed my Navy career to give our new marriage a fighting chance. Now you have the nerve to open your mouth and say, "I don't want to be married anymore." He had the nerve to tell me that one woman wasn't enough for him and that he could have any woman he wanted.

As a veteran, I can concur with him. Imagine you're a young handsome man in the military with good benefits, having a guaranteed paycheck every first and fifteen of the month. This makes a man a commodity. You'll be surprised how many women in America and internationally see these men as a come up and a golden ticket out of a tough situation. There were several embarrassing visits to medical because I contracted venereal diseases from him whenever he came home after being deployed overseas. I thank God for the pillow fights and the screaming I did. I cried so many tears because I did everything the church mothers told me to do. I anointed his zippers and shoes. I poured holy oil in his mouth while he slept and I even lathered his head with it. Yet he still wanted a divorce and all I encumbered had taken a toll on my heart. I became so consumed with anger that I became bitter and very vengeful. I made numerous calls to his commander and supervisors, trying to end his career to no avail. I would envision myself killing him and I remember preparing to go incognito to his barracks and wait for him. God knew what was in my heart and would not let my car start so I thanked Him later for divine intervention.

The fury I had for my ex-husband manifested in other areas of my life. It affected the way I treated my brothers in Christ. They called me Sister Ice and I was a tyrant to those I supervised in the military. I was making every man inadvertently pay for what my ex-husband did to me. I remember a brother in Christ came to me after church service and with tears in his eyes, he asked me why I hated him and men in general. I didn't answer and he told me, "Sister Taylor, I love you and I'm praying for God to take away your anger." I didn't expect that and on my way home, I had a full conversation with myself. I believe what he said was imparted in my spirit. I can't tell you when or how soon afterwards, but this scripture resonated in my spirit, *Romans 12:17-19 KJV, "Recompense to no man evil for evil. Provide things honest in the sight of all men. If it be possible as much as lieth in you, live peaceably with all men. Dearly beloved, avenge not yourselves, but rather give place unto wrath: for it is written, Vengeance is mine; I will repay, saith the Lord."* I began to notice how I treated my male coworkers and brothers in Christ and honestly speaking, my behavior didn't change overnight. But what did change is that I prayed for God to take away my anger and to give up control in wanting to get even.

CHAPTER FOUR

"Can We Try Again?" - Bargaining

Oxford Languages defines bargain as the following:

1. to part with something after negotiation,
2. be prepared for;
3. expect.

4. to exchange goods or services without using money,

5. to negotiate the terms.

In simple terms, to bargain is to barter or make a deal and agree. In the Bible there are several who were skilled in bargaining. Abraham, Moses, and Jesus Christ all interceded on behalf of the people. For example, have you ever visited a farmer's market? If yes, then you see bargaining in action. There's a set price for an item and you, the buyer, propose a lower price to the seller. There will be an exchange between the seller and the buyer until both agree on the amount, and both are happy. So, the bargaining stage is often referred to as a defense mechanism. You're desperate and want everything to return to normal. You'll find yourself trying to negotiate with God, the other person, and yourself.

I told myself, "I'll dress more seductively, go to the clubs with him and be everything he wanted me to be." I went and bought a bunch of sexy lingerie. I even told God that if He restored my marriage, I would be a better wife. I had many invading thoughts of everything I did wrong and what I should've done better. I am pleading with God that I'll pray and fast more in exchange if He restored my marriage. I kept my end of the deal, and I was always fasting, but nothing changed. I was on an emotional roller coaster at this stage. I had anxiety, guilt, and fear. All these emotions were directed internally and externally towards my spouse and all men. I felt like I failed as a woman because I couldn't keep him satisfied. I was anxious about how people viewed me and afraid because I was alone. During this time in my life, I was plagued by fear, and I had a strong need to feel protected or safe. So, in bargaining, reality hadn't quite set in and by trying to change my present in exchange for something better, I included my ex in the picture. It kept me in protective mode, but then I realized nothing wasn't changing in my favor except that all the fasting and praying made me stronger and developed a more intimate relationship with God, which kept me.

CHAPTER FIVE

"Rainy Days"- Depression

I can tell you a thing or two about depression. It seemed like I was stuck in this stage for an eternity. First, let's define depression. According to Oxford Language, depression is:

1. Unresolved anger.

2. A mood disorder that causes a persistent feeling of sadness and loss of interest and can affect how you feel, think, and behave.

Several Bible figures dealt with depression and or mental health issues at some point in their life. I often studied their lives, what they went through, and how they overcame their low state in life. Thus, I'm sharing with you in hopes you will be uplifted in knowing you are not alone.

1. **David-** He dealt with guilt, loss, and fear. *(Psalms 6:6, Psalms 42:11)*
2. **Elijah-** Emotional Burnout, Fear and Hopelessness *(1 Kings 19:4)*
3. **Hannah-** Grief, Weeping, Anguish, and Mocked *(1 Samuel 1:1-20)*
4. **Jeremiah-** Weeping Prophet, Loneliness, Rejection, Failure- *(Jeremiah 20:18)*
5. **Jonah-** Anger and Suicidal *(Jonah 4)*
6. **Moses-** Anger, Discouraged, and Rejection *(Exodus 4:18)*
7. **Job-** Grief, Loss *(Job 1: 1-42)*

In the bargaining stage, I didn't get the anticipated results, and the fact that my marriage was at a conclusion and divorce was a certainty. The breath was knocked out of me and all I could do was cry. I cried so much that I remember a Prophet called me out and said, "Sister Taylor, every time I see You, you're always crying." I often found myself vacillating with anger and bargaining. So, in this stage, I was very irrational. One moment, I was trying to make a deal with God and the next second, I was full of explosive anger and wanted to really hurt my ex. I went from being a confident, well-groomed woman to an unkempt woman with low self-esteem. I would always keep my head lowered to the ground and at this time, no one knew I was abusing myself physically. I would have scratches and bruising on my body, especially on my face. I pulled chunks of my hair out. I was anorexic and bulimic. I even gave myself blackeyes that I covered with makeup.

My pastor, at the time, became a father to me. I would call him and ask, "Who am I?" He would tell me my name and something about myself. In the Navy, I was a jet mechanic. Sometimes, my mind would go blank when I would arrive at work. I would sit in the locker room and pray for my mind to return. In nursing school, the teacher would be lecturing, and my mind would leave, and I had to pretend I was okay. On good days, I would write notes to myself like:

- How to brush my teeth
- How to open and close the door
- How to get in and out of the car
- Directions to and from work and home

My mind was gone. I would forget my name, where I lived, and how to do the simplest tasks. In Washington State, there was a bridge called Deception Pass and many people jumped off this bridge. I remember driving to it one night. I got out of my car, stood in front of it, and heard this voice saying loudly, "Jump! Jump!" I was being drawn by the waves of the water then I heard the horn of a car, and it was like I came out of a daze. I got in my car and drove back to my barracks. I would pace the floors for hours till the bottom of my feet hurt. I would hang dark blankets over my windows. I thought people were trying to take pictures of me because I would hear the flashing of a camera. My job performance and relationships were hindered.

I dealt with depression, self-abuse, and suicidal ideations for about two years. I attended a church service, where Evangelist Dorinda Clark was the guest speaker and she called me out of the audience. I went forward and she spoke these simple words to me, *"Weeping may endureth for the night but joy cometh in the morning (Psalms 30:5)."* She told me that I didn't have to wait for the morning and that I could have Joy Now! I chose Joy in that instance. Those words broke something in me and were the catalyst for my healing.

I was led by God to study about the anointing and the woman who had the spirit of infirmity, whose spine was stuck together for eighteen years and nothing she did helped. But one day, Jesus was in the sanctuary, and He called her forward and she was loosed from her infirmity because of the anointing *(Luke 13:10-13).*

The Holy Spirit would have me read clean jokes and the comics in the newspaper. I bought coloring books and colored. I played games like Jacks and Hop Scotch, which I enjoyed as a child. I read the book of Psalms and did all these things to bring some type of laughter and joy to my life to counterattack the heaviness and hopelessness I felt. The Holy Spirit was teaching me to laugh again, and, on several occasions, I would be on the floor in my living room and bedroom, having belly-aching laughter and tears rolling down my eyes.

Proverbs 17:22 says, "A merry heart doeth good like medicine: but a broken spirit drieth the bones." I was being healed through His holy laughter. My God has a sense of humor; no one could tell me otherwise. After studying about the woman with the issue of blood and the woman with the spirit of infirmity, I began to feel a difference in my spirit. The Lord told me to call the pastor and ask him if I could bring the word at church. The pastor said yes, and I was given a date. Mind you, during this time, I was in a place of brokenness and hadn't been coming to church, but I kept communicating with my leader. That's why it's so important to be under the right God-appointed leadership.

My leader knew my spirit and the God in me. As the shepherd, he knew where I was spiritually, and he also heard from God. Without going into detail because that's for another book, I will say, however, that the day I spoke, my message was titled, *"Naked and Not Ashamed,"* and another well-known preacher at the time was known for this message. God had me bring it forth from another perspective. The glory fell and many people were delivered. The spirit of oppression was broken off my life because of the anointing. It was at that moment while ministering, it began to all make sense. My pain had purpose and I needed to tell my story without shame, and I couldn't do it bound in depression.

CHAPTER SIX:

"It Is What It Is"- Acceptance

"Not that I speak in respect of want for I have learned, in whatsoever state I am, therewith to be content." — *(Philippians 4:11 KJV)*

Oxford Languages defines acceptance as the ability to acknowledge the reality of a situation without resistance. Recognizes that it is what it is. Paul was a prisoner en route to prison on a ship and along the way, he encountered a monstrous storm. Everyone aboard was afraid they were going to die. God spoke to Paul and he reassured everyone that they wouldn't die if they stayed in the boat. They are shipwrecked and Paul arrives at a place called Malta, which means honey sweet. The men arrived on broken pieces of the ship *(Acts 28:3-5)*.

To get warm, Paul gathers wood and starts a fire. The heat brings a viper out of the wood. The poisonous snake bites his hand and Paul shakes it off into the fire and he's unharmed. The other men expect Paul to die but he doesn't. The monstrous storm symbolizes that sometimes we will encounter horrific things in life, and it makes no sense to us. Arriving on broken pieces means God will intervene on our behalf and bring us to a place that is honey sweet. You can learn from every trial. I think of the scripture, *Romans 8:28, "And we know that all things work together for good to them that love God, to them who are called according to his purpose."*

It is in Malta, a sweet place where, although Paul is a prisoner, he had many liberties. It was a beautiful scenic place. He could have visitors and ate the best of foods. He even had favor with jailers, for they liked Paul and there wasn't anything they would not do for Paul within reason. This was the place he wrote most of his letters to the church. There's beauty in our brokenness and we see it in this case. Paul was content because he trusted God. He learned to trust in God, and it was for a greater call. He knew his life was in the hands of the Almighty and he was able to make the most of his present circumstance. Centuries later, his contribution to the Bible encourages every believer today. To reiterate, the venomous snake bit Paul and he wasn't harmed. I think of a saying the old people used to say, "What doesn't kill you will only make you stronger."

The summation of my marriage was very painful, and I thought my heart would never heal. There's an old movie that starred Doris Day titled, *"With Six You Get Egg Rolls"* in which she plays a married woman with several children and a stay-at-home mom. Her husband is the typical bread winner. This movie was circa the 1950's and this was the normal. Later, she becomes a widow and is left to fend for her kids and home with no skills and limited money. At first, you find her always crying and retrospectively, you see her going through the five stages of grief.

There was a hit song that Doris Day sang called, *"Que Sera Sera,"* which means "whatever will be, will be." This song was fitting, especially during those hard moments in her life. She eventually gets to a place where she's content and at peace because she embraced her situation. Ironically, many years later, I too would sing it at the end of my marriage. Honestly, this is not what I wanted but I knew I would be okay. My acceptance helped stabilize my emotions instead of being driven by them. Although "My Forever and Always," no longer existed, I welcomed my new reality in knowing that God would never leave nor forsake me and that He'll love me for a lifetime.

Hebrews 13:5 says, "For he hath said, I will never leave thee, nor forsake thee."

Matthew 28:20 says, "And lo, I am with you always, even unto the end of the world. Amen."

In the Book of Ruth, Naomi loses everything: her husband, covering, sons, provision, legacy, and the ability to be a grandmother. She lost all hope and returned to her land, Judah, with her daughter-in-law Ruth. Everyone is so excited to see her.

Ruth 1:20-21 says, "And she said unto them, "Call me Mara: for the Almighty hath dealt with me very bitterly with me. I went out full and the Lord hath brought me home again empty: why then call me Naomi, seeing the Lord hath testified against me, and the Almighty hath afflicted me?"

Naomi had lost all faith and became embittered by her losses. She was angry with God and wanted to be called what she felt. At this point, Naomi is embedded in the stages of anger and depression. Happily, we later see that Naomi worked through the stages of grief and came to a place of acceptance. She undertakes her detriments as power and hope is rekindled.

Jeremiah 29:11 says, "For I know the thoughts I think towards you, saith the Lord, thoughts of peace, and not of evil, to give you an expected end."

Naomi began to see the perfect plan of God unfold right before her eyes and she began to trust God again. With this new insight, she tells Ruth that Boaz is a relative and a protector and gives her Godly counsel. Both of their lives were restored through the marriage of Boaz and Ruth. God turned their rainy days to days full of sunshine.

CHAPTER SEVEN

"Anchored" - Hope

"Which hope we have as an anchor of the soul, both sure and steadfast, and which entereth into that within the veil." — *(Hebrews 6:19 KJV)*

According to Oxford Languages, hope is a feeling of expectation and desire for a certain thing to happen. It is also a feeling of trust. Acceptance brought a sense of renewed desire in my life. I sang a song that became my anthem,

"Trouble Don't Last Always." Jesus became my in-
spiration and an anchor to me. Just like a ship
being tossed back and forth by the turbulence of
moving waters and storms. By staying connected
to Jesus I wouldn't be moved. I also knew without
Him I would be like a ship without a sail. In Jesus,
I remained steadfast and unmovable despite the
tides of life.

*Psalms 18:6 says, "I have always set the Lord
before me; because He is at my right hand, I shall
not be moved."* It's like springtime that brings
expectation, excitement of what will bloom or
spring forth. The budding or the coming forth of
what's been planted is symbolic of a new thing, a
new season and the past is left behind. It's over.
*"Behold, the former things are come to pass, and new
things do I declare before they spring forth, I tell you
of them (Isaiah 42:9)."* So its true trouble doesn't
last always. It was like spring was in the air and
life was full of new possibilities. I went back to
school for nursing, travelled, started two busi-
nesses, and got lost in ministry.

There's a childhood character called, Annie
who was an orphan who suffered many hardships

and would sing a song called, *"It's the Hard-Knock Life."* Life in the orphanage was full of hard labor, food scarcity and the basic life essentials were little to none. She was mistreated by adults, especially by those in authority. Annie's life changed when she was adopted by someone who really loved her. Her song became a happy song called, *"Tomorrow."* It was about how the sun will come out tomorrow and it's only a day away. It's a song about how things have a way of changing for the better. Annie's life was changed for the better and she wanted others to never stop believing.

In the beginning of my grief process, I asked a question that I couldn't answer because where I was in my pain. That question was, "What's Next God?," with a longing to continue and see what the end will be. Now I can answer the question and it is Live, Live, Live!!!

CHAPTER EIGHT

The Conversations

"*Thy testimonies also my delight and my counsel-ors.*" — *(Psalms 119:24 KJV)*

In this chapter I will anonymously share tes-timonies and wisdom nuggets of two of my cous-ins in their grieving process. Lady Oak disclosed that she went from her parent's house at eighteen years of age to her husband's house. She became a wife, and mother and that's all she knew. With all her children grown and out of the house, this is the first time in her life she's been alone. She states, "It is like being single and for the first time, I don't have to cook unless I want to, and if I want to lay around all day I can." She made it noticeably clear she feels like a part of her is missing. She was married fifty plus years. Mrs. Oak is travelling, working part time, learning modern technology, and even speaking at church. God is breaking so many negative cycles in her life. She is coming into her own identity because sometimes in marriage, you lose a sense of self, and it's so liberating. After the death of her spouse, she asked God, "Why am I still here?" and "What's Next God?" God answered her through prophecy that she was still needed, and that God has work for her to do. She has accepted this and has made up in her mind.... "I'm going to live if I have breath in my lungs."

Lady Dee stated the following: I lost my husband unexpectantly and I didn't have closure and honestly, I stayed in shock and anger for a longer than I should of. I was angry because my husband died, and I was angry with God that He took someone who was good to me. I put on a strong face but baby behind closed doors, I was an emotional wreck. It was through my children and grandchildren that helped push me through the stages of grief because they needed me and checking out wasn't an option.

Matthew 5:4 says, "Blessed are they that mourn for they shall be comforted." I found comfort in strengthening my relationships, especially with family. Slowly I began to smile again and knew this too shall pass and with each passing day, I was stronger. I was able to let go of the anger, and I realized God needed my husband more than me.

Both ladies shared the importance of making a bucket list of things they always wanted to do but never had the chance to do. They also shared wisdom nuggets of what they learned in their process of healing. I also did a bucket of my passions after my divorce which helped me to be excited about life again. I would say to make a bucket list with at least ten things and accomplish them.

WISDOM NUGGETS:

1. Allow yourself to go through the process but don't stay there, whether it's anger or depression. Keep it Moving.
2. Take the time to get to know yourself.
3. All Eyes are on you, so be selfish about you.
4. Go to a movie or dinner by yourself. You are an interesting person.
5. Get out the bed and out of the house and live!

CHAPTER NINE

Biblical References

Jesus, Anna, David, Ruth all dealt with diffi-cult losses of loved ones and each one managed their grief differently in their own way. Some got stuck and some became bitter. They however went through the stages of grief for a season and they continued with life.

JESUS

Matthew 14:13-14 says, "When Jesus heard of it, he departed thence by ship into a desert place apart: and when the people had heard thereof, they followed him on foot out of the cities. And Jesus went forth, and saw a great multitude, he was moved with compassion toward them, and he healed their sick."

Jesus was told about the death of John the Baptist, his cousin and forerunner who prepared the way for his arrival. Jesus went to a solitary place, a place without people, and took the time to grieve the loss of John. Thus, Jesus showed us that it is essential to grieve and that we must allow ourselves to be comforted in our time of mourning.

Matthew 5:4 KJV says, "Blessed are they that mourned, for they shall be comforted."

In this isolated place, Jesus is praying and communing with God. In the meantime, the people sought him out on foot thus symbolizing that it took them some time to locate Jesus. When the people arrived, he completed his grieving process. He saw the people, was moved with compassion, and healed the sick. Further, in *Matthew Chapter 5,* Jesus also feeds the crowd. Jesus displays that it's okay to grieve but do not get stuck. Stay focused, continue in life, and finish your assignment.

ANNA

Luke 2:36-38 KJV says, "And there was one Anna, a prophetess, the daughter of Phanuel, of the tribe of Asher: she was of a great age, and she lived with a husband seven years from her virginity; And she now a widow of about fourscore years, which departed not from the temple, but served God with fastings and prayers night and day. And she coming in that instant gave thanks likewise unto the Lord, and spake of him to all of them that looked for redemption in Jerusalem."

Anna (whose name means God, who has favored me) was the daughter of Phanuel (whose name means the face of God), who was a descendant of the tribe of Asher (which means happy and blessed). Anna was married at an early age, approximately 14 years old and was widowed seven years later and had no children conceived. She was considered old and barren, which made marriage prospects very slim. Widows were seen as a burden and lived off the charities of people. She was in a situation where she was shunned and looked down upon.

Anna remembered growing up in a household and surrounded by happy people and abundance. The tribe of Asher were called a happy and blessed people because they made their wealth through cultivating olive oil, which symbolizes abundance, divine grace, peace, spiritual wisdom, restoration, and healing. Her father, Phanuel, was a significant figure in her life. He represented the face of God, and his constant presence brought her joy.

Psalms 16:11 says, "In thy presence is fullness of joy."

Anna sought out joy and peace by seeking the place where God abided. She found solace in the temple of God and as she drew near to God, he drew closer to her *(Psalms 119:92)*. It was in the temple, where she experienced the face of God through her sacrifices of fasting and worship. Anna was healed of her grief and in exchange, she was joyful for her tears and her mourning was turned into dancing.

Anna was made strong by God. On every occasion, she would tell everyone who visited the temple about the Messiah who would come and bring deliverance. Anna's diligence positioned her to witness Jesus's arrival. Anna's grief process encourages us that healing comes by staying in the presence of God and if we seek Him, we will find Him.

DAVID

2 Samuel 12:15-23 KJV tells a story of David, Bathsheba, and Nathan and the consequences of sin. Starting at verse 19, *"But when David saw that his servants whispered, David perceived that the child was dead: therefore, David said unto his servants, Is the child dead? And they said, "He is dead. The house: arose from the earth, and washed, and anointed himself, and changed his apparel, and came into the house of the Lord, and worshipped: then he came to his own house; and when required, they set bread before him, and he did eat. And he said, While the child was alive, I fasted and wept: for I said, Who can tell whether God will be gracious to me, that the child may live? But now he is dead, wherefore should I fast? Can I bring him back again? I shall go to him, but he shall not return to me."*

The prophet Nathan tells David of his sin that the child he made with Bathsheba will not live. The child becomes sick and David goes into fasting and crying out for God's mercy while prostrate on the ground. On the seventh day, he hears that the child has died. David gets up, bathes, changes his clothes, and eats. His servant does not understand how he shifted from weeping to continuing with life. David says that if God were going to intervene, He would have done it. So therefore, David is in a place of acceptance and can move on with life. He returns to his own house thus symbolizing that he has finished grieving and lays with Bathsheba. As a result, Solomon was conceived. This scenario implies that hope has been restored and David looks forward to the future and what life will bring him. David was acceptant of his loss. He was able to embrace that God is in control and can be trusted.

RUTH

Ruth 1: 16-17 KJV says, " And Ruth said, Intreat me not to leave thee, or return from following after thee: for wither thou goest, I will go; and where thou lodgest, I will lodge: thy people shall be my people, and thy God my God: Where thou diest, I will die, and there will I be buried: the Lord do so to me, and more also, if ought but death part thee and me."

Naomi loses her husband and later both her sons. She hears that God is blessing his people in Judah and plans to return. Her daughters-in-law wanted to accompany her. She reminded them to return to their people because they were no longer under marital obligations. Naomi also tells them that she can't provide a future for them because she doesn't see herself getting married again and having more children. She loved them too much to wait for them to grow up and marry. Orpah returns to her hometown.

Ruth, which means a compassionate friend, couldn't abandon Naomi and vowed that she would follow her wherever she went and that her people and God would become hers as well. Ruth, a Moabite who was reared and familiar with gods, had been exposed to the God of Bethlehem through stories told by her in-laws. She wanted to go to Judah, a place where God was restoring and had hope for a better future. She goes to Bethlehem (house of God) and adheres to the wise counsel of Ruth. She works in the fields gleaning, and despite the harshness of it, she is faithful.

The gleaning of the harvest symbolizes that although going through the process of grief can be painful, if you continue in it, there will be fruit. Ruth was vulnerable but Boaz noticed her working and provided safety. Ruth was a woman of God and chose to follow God rather than go back to what was familiar to her, which was idol worship. Thus, she becomes the key contributor to Naomi's life being healed naturally and spiritually. Ruth became a faithful friend to a woman overtaken in sorrow and through this connection, she said yes to hope and faith, which represents abiding loyalty and devotion.

Proverbs 3:5 KJV says, "Trust in the Lord with all thine heart; and lean not to thine own understanding."

Ruth loved Naomi and didn't want to abandon her in her low state, for they had developed a close relationship with each other. During her marriage to Mahlon, she heard many stories of their God and his mighty acts. Curiosity had risen in her heart, and she knew He was where Naomi was going and that is where she went. She was barren and a widow, and she was healed and restored because of her faithfulness. Her pain produced fruitfulness, a son of which Jesus was a descendant. Everything she lost was restored and she and Naomi were made happy again.

About The Author

Sandra L. Ross is an ordained Prophetess, Intercessor, Teacher, and a Poet. She is the author of "*It's Raining Wisdom: The Golden Nuggets of God,*" "*Healing Waters: Poems That Heal,*" "*Let's Tell A Story: The Allegories of God,*" *and* "*God Is.*" Sandra has served in multiple areas of ministry, but her greatest love is for the broken-hearted and those bound by pain from their past. Sandra is a true witness of the wonder-working power of God in her life. Sandra experienced the ugliness of abuse and all it entails. She lived life as a victim. But one day, she heard the words, "It's not in vain." With this new perspective, her life was never the same. No longer walking in shame, her mourning was turned into dancing, and she was given beauty for ashes. Formerly a victim, Sandra is now a survivor because her wounds did not kill her but birthed in her a passion to see people released from the prisons of their pain and to be made whole.

Citations

1. Chapter One- OxfordLanguages.com
2. Chapter Two- HealthCentral.com – "The Five Stages of Grief – An Examination of the Kubler-Ross Model 06/07/2022 Marisa M. Tomasic, PHD. Vocabulary. com, WebMd.com/depression/depression-grief, Health.Harvard.edu- Harvard Heath Publishing Harvard Medical School Five Stages of Grief: Coping with the loss Who Struggled with Depression by Debbie McDaniel 03/08/2021, reclaimToday.

com- Six People in the bible who struggled with their mental health 01/19/2024 In Wellness Mental Health Anxious Faith

3. Chapter Six- OxfordLanguages.com, Health.Harvard.edu

4. Chapter Seven-OxfordLanguages.com

YOU WILL LIVE AND YOU WILL THRIVE

Index

A

Emotional Burnout, 19

emotional roller coaster, 17

emotions, 4, 10, 17, 28

eternity, 18

Evangelist Dorinda Clark, 21

event, 1, 6

evil, 14, 29

excursions, 7

ex-husband, 8, 12, 13

expectation, 31, 32

Ezra, 5, 6, 7, 9

F

Failure, 19

faith, 29, 45

faithfulness, 46

family, 36

farmer's market, 16

fasting, 17, 42, 43

father, 20, 41

favor, 17, 27

fear, 17, 19

financial stressors, 1

fire, 26

five stages of grief, 2, 3, 4, 28

Hannah, 19

happy, 16, 33, 40, 41, 46

hard labor, 33

hardships, 32

harvest, 45

Hawaii, 12

head, 5, 6, 13, 20

healing, 22, 36, 41, 42

Healing Waters, 47

heart, 6, 9, 10, 13, 23, 27, 45, 46

heaviness, 22

Hebrew, 6

help, 6

helper, 6

hips, 12

holiness, 6, 7

holy oil, 13

Holy Spirit, 8, 9, 22

home, 7, 8, 13, 14, 21, 27, 29

hometown, 44

honest, 14

Hop Scotch, 22

hope, 29, 31, 43, 45

Hopelessness, 19

hostility, 11

house, 10, 34, 35, 37, 42, 43, 45